SMART HOUSE
CRAF KIDS

...OUND PROJECTS
OLIDAYS,
RTIES,
nd MORE ....

LLY DIXON ·

DATE DUE

MAR 2 7 2018	
SEP 1 5 2018	

BRODART, CO.   Cat. No. 23-221

PLAIN

AN IMPRINT O

SPRINGVILLE, UTAH

ISBN 13: 978-1-4621-1542-6

Published by Plain Sight Publishing, an imprint of Cedar Fort, Inc.
2373 W. 700 S., Springville, UT 84663
Distributed by Cedar Fort, Inc., www.cedarfort.com

LIBRARY OF CONGRESS CATALOGING-IN-PUBLICATION DATA
Dixon, Kelly, 1983- author.
Smart school house crafts for kids / Kelly Dixon.
    pages cm
Summary: Educational crafts that include step-by-step instructions for preschool and elementary-aged children.
ISBN 978-1-4621-1542-6 (alk. paper)
1. Handicraft. 2. Creative activities and seat work--Handbooks, manuals, etc. 3. Early childhood education--Activity programs. I. Title.

TT157.D587 2015
745.5--dc23

                    2014039563

Cover design by M. Shaun McMurdie and Lauren Error
Page design by M. Shaun McMurdie
Cover design © 2015 Lyle Mortimer
Edited and typeset by Deborah Spencer and Eileen Leavitt

Printed in China

10 9 8 7 6 5 4 3 2 1

Printed on acid-free paper

Contents

Winter

EDIBLE COOKIE PAINT

With cold days outside and lots of busy hands in the kitchen, this fun winter cookie-decorating project with edible cookie paint is a favorite in our house. Who knew that ingredients as simple as marshmallows and a little bit of corn syrup could turn an afternoon into a fun family event? The texture is smooth and soft, the colors are vibrant, and your cookies will taste delicious! When the magical ingredients are combined, you get a perfectly smooth paint that is ready to paint onto holiday sugar cookies.

Supplies Needed

- mini marshmallows
- water
- light corn syrup
- food coloring
- watercolor paint brushes
- paper

Directions

1. Put 1 cup of mini marshmallows in a microwave-safe bowl, and microwave them for 30 seconds. The marshmallows will expand. (It's really cool!)

2. Add ¼ cup of water to the microwaved marshmallows. Stir the water into the marshmallows. The marshmallows will continue to melt.

3. Put the mixture in the microwave again for 30 more seconds.

4. Add 3 tablespoons of light corn syrup to the marshmallow-water mixture, and stir it in well.

5. Microwave it again for 30 seconds.

Directions Continued

6. Stir it together until every bit of the marsh-mallows are melted and mixed well with the corn syrup.

7. Let it cool just a tad, and then separate it into different containers.

8. Using a drop of coloring at a time, make whatever colors you desire! I suggest craft popsicle sticks to stir up the paint colors.

9. The paint will be hot! Let it cool for 2 minutes (or until warm) before using.

10. Using small paint brushes, decorate the holiday cookies. The paint will dry within a few hours, and it tastes fantastically fun on top of sugar cookies!

CANDY CANE SUGAR SCRUB

Sugar scrubs are incredibly fun to make, smell fantastic, and leave your hands feeling super soft! Best of all, they make a wonderful gift for friends, family, and teachers. Candy Cane Sugar Scrub is one of my very favorite sugar scrub recipes. You can separate the sugar scrub into small containers and hand them out for the holidays, or you can keep it all for yourself. It is a festive way to keep your skin soft during the cold winter months.

Supplies Needed

- baby oil
- Dr. Bronner's peppermint castile soap (liquid)
- white sugar
- plastic or glass jar(s)
- red-and-white baker's twine
- mini candy cane

Directions

1. Combine ¼ cup of baby oil with ¼ cup of Dr. Bronner's peppermint castile soap.

2. Add in 2½ cups of white sugar. If you like a smoother sugar scrub, add less sugar. If you like a fluffier sugar scrub, add in a little more sugar.

3. Put the sugar scrub into a container with a lid.

4. Using the baker's twine, tie a mini candy cane onto the outside of your jar.

FIND THE PRINTABLE AT
CEDARFORTBOOKS.COM/SMARTSCHOOLHOUSE

Winter

CHRISTMAS MILK CUP COVERS

If Santa (and Santa's helpers) are holding out for a fun Christmas treat, we've got you covered—literally. Print these adorable Christmas Milk Covers, cut them out, punch or press a hole in the center, and place a straw inside to keep the covers in place. They are also fun to use for holiday parties or snack time with friends, so be sure you make one for yourself, and don't leave all of the fun to Santa!

SURPRISINGLY BOUNCY SNOWBALLS

Have you ever seen snow bounce? Well now you will! These sparkly snowballs are surprisingly bouncy, and they are also fun to make! The bouncy balls will stay in the form of a ball while you are playing with them, but if you stack them up or set them down, they will slowly melt together! Your guests and friends will have a blast playing with these fabulously frosty-looking winter snowballs!

Supplies Needed

- measuring spoons
- warm water
- borax
- 2 disposable cups (or small glass bowls)
- white glue
- cornstarch
- clear or white glitter
- plastic spoon
- ziplock plastic bag

— NOTE FOR GROWN-UPS —

Borax should be handled by adults and can be harmful if ingested. So be careful, and keep it away from young children or animals that might try to eat it.

Directions

1. Pour 2 tablespoons of warm water and ½ teaspoon borax powder into 1 disposable cup. Carefully stir the mixture until the borax is completely dissolved. This is your borax cup.

2. In a separate disposable cup, combine 1 tablespoon of glue, 1 tablespoon of cornstarch, and ½ teaspoon of the solution from the borax cup.

3. Let the ingredients sit for 30 seconds.

4. Using a plastic spoon, stir together the mixture.

5. Mix in 1 tablespoon of glitter.

6. When the mixture becomes too difficult to stir with a plastic spoon, pick it up out of the cup, and begin mixing it by hand.

Directions Continued

7. Play with the mixture in your hands until it takes on a solid form.

8. Once it is solid, roll it in some additional glitter (optional), and then bounce it on the table!

9. When you're done playing, store the snowballs in a ziplock bag.

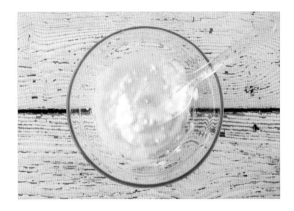

APPLE JUICE BOTTLE SNOW GLOBE

Winter is the season for making snow globes! More than one hundred years ago, people used to make snow globes out of clear glass balls. Inside, there would be a very tiny village scene, and when you shook the ball, small white particles inside the glass ball would move around so it looked like snow was falling on the tiny miniature village. This snow globe doesn't look like snow at all, but you will have lots of fun shaking it up and watching what happens inside. Snow globes can be decorated in a variety of different ways, and this one is extra sparkly, which is part of what makes it fun to play with! This project also doubles as a stress-reliever as you watch the sparkling jewels inside float and weave. What a calming way to end a busy day.

Supplies Needed

- empty apple-shaped apple juice jar
- corn syrup
- food coloring
- glitter, diamonds, or various craft supplies
- superglue (for parents)

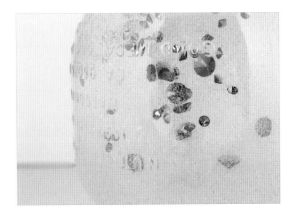

Directions

1. Clean out the inside of an apple juice bottle.

2. Pour corn syrup into the apple juice jar until it is almost full. That little bit of air at the top will allow the objects on the inside to move once it is sealed.

3. Put glitter, jewels, food coloring, beads, and whatever craft supplies you like into the jar.

4. Using superglue, seal the lid of the apple juice jar shut, and allow it to dry completely.

Directions Continued

5. Rotate the snow globe from side to side or rest it on a flat surface. Watch the inside slowly move around, creating fun and relaxing scenes!

STEPS 1 AND 2

STEP 3

STEP 4

FIND THE PRINTABLE AT
CEDARFORTBOOKS.COM/SMARTSCHOOLHOUSE

Winter

BE MINE VALENSLIME

Slime is one of the coolest crafts to make! It's gooey, slippery, and cold. Because slime has qualities of both a solid and a liquid, it will stay in a particular shape for a few moments before melting back into a slime puddle. Slime can be made in a variety of colors, and it makes a really fun gift. For this activity, we will make some Valentine's Day slime that you can give to friends or classmates on Valentine's Day!

Supplies Needed

- 2 bowls
- measuring cup and measuring spoons
- water
- borax
- 1 (4-oz.) bottle of white school glue
- pink and blue food coloring
- small plastic containers with lids
- "Be Mine ValenSlime" printable tags
- double-sided tape

Directions

1. In one bowl, combine 1 cup of water with 1 teaspoon of borax.

2. In a second bowl, pour out the entire 4-oz. bottle of white school glue. Mix ½ cup of water into the glue.

3. Add in a few drops of either pink or blue food coloring. Stir the glue, water, and food coloring until completely combined.

4. Pour the first bowl of borax and water into the second bowl of the colored glue mixture.

5. Using your hands, knead the mixture together for about 3 minutes.

6. Pour the extra water down the sink.

— NOTE FOR GROWN-UPS —

Borax should be handled by adults and can be harmful if ingested. So be careful, and keep it away from young children or animals that might try to eat it.

Directions Continued

7. Continue to play with the gooey slime until it all sticks together.

8. Separate the slime into small plastic containers and seal with a lid.

9. Repeat steps 1–8 using a different food coloring.

10. Print out the various "Be Mine ValenSlime" tags and, using double-sided tape, attach the ValenSlime tags to the lids of the small plastic containers.

11. The slime will stay fresh and gooey as long as it is kept in airtight containers. It will provide hours of playtime!

STEP 3

STEP 3

STEP 3–4

STEP 8

YOU

MY HEART

UP ♥

FIND THE PRINTABLE AT
CEDARFORTBOOKS.COM/SMARTSCHOOLHOUSE

Winter

YOU BLOW MY HEART UP—A BUBBLE GUM VALENTINE

This bubble-licious Valentine's Day craft is incredibly fun to give to friends or teachers on Valentine's Day! Valentine's Day is a day to celebrate those you love, and handmade gifts from the heart are an extra special way to show someone that you care. Gumballs are colorful, sweet, and cute, which makes them perfect for embellishing gifts. For this craft, you will need gumballs and a few other items that you can pick up from a craft store. You will also need a hot glue gun for this particular Valentine's Day activity, so parent supervision and help is important!

Supplies Needed

- 2 sheets of red craft foam
- scissors
- pencil
- X-ACTO knife (optional)
- gumballs
- hot glue gun
- plastic bag (sandwich size)
- string
- "You Blow My Heart Up" printable tags

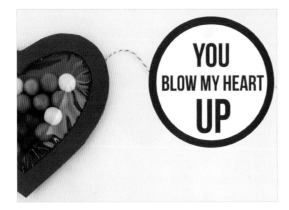

Directions

1. Cut a heart shape out of red craft foam that is slightly smaller than the size of your plastic bag. (We'll refer to this as the *base heart*.)

2. Trace around the edges of the base heart on another sheet of red craft foam.

3. Cut out the second heart. It will be the same size as the first heart.

4. Make a frame with this second heart-shaped piece of craft foam by cutting a smaller heart shape out of the center, leaving a 1-inch-wide "frame." Parents can do the cutting with an X-ACTO knife or by simply pressing scissors through the second heart and cutting along the outside edge.

5. Place gumballs on the base heart.

6. A grown-up can help you quickly draw a line of hot glue halfway around the outside edge of the base heart.

7. Have a grown-up place the plastic bag on top of the hot glue. The hot glue will melt both layers of the plastic bag onto the foam base.

8. Repeat steps 6–7 for the opposite half of the base heart. When cooled, the entire bag should be sealed down tight.

9. Using scissors, trim off all of the extra plastic that extends over the edge of the base heart from the bag.

10. Place a small piece of string on the outside edge of the bag. (This will be used to hold the printable Valentine's tag.)

11. Using hot glue, attach the heart frame to the heart base, sealing in the string, the plastic bag, and the bubble gum.

12. Print out a "You Blow My Heart Up" bubble gum printable tag, and glue it to the end of your string.

STEPS 1 AND 3

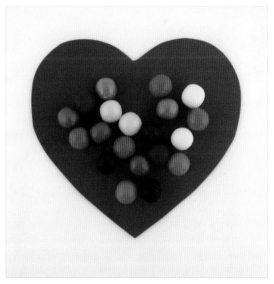

STEP 5

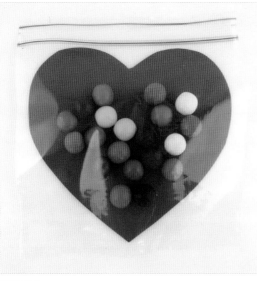

STEP 7-8

STEP 9

STEP 10–11

STEP 10–11

Winter

STEP 12

FIND THE PRINTABLE AT
CEDARFORTBOOKS.COM/SMARTSCHOOLHOUSE

ABC FOAM CHAINS

Winter

A fun way to learn the ABCs or to practice spelling words is to make reusable foam chains. The chains can be made into any color you want! What I love about these ABC Foam Chains is that they can be used in so many different ways. You can make extra-long, goofy words or practice letter-blending sounds. They can help with spelling words, or they can help with simple letter recognition. Kids love building paper chains, so making reusable foam chains to play and learn with is so smart!

Supplies Needed

- various colored sheets of craft foam
- scissors
- sticky-back Velcro circles
- "ABC Foam Chains" printable letters
- glue or sticky paper

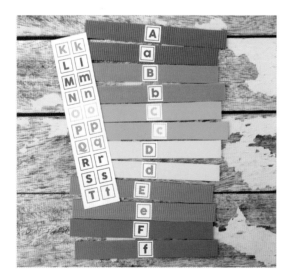

Directions

1. Cut the various strips of colored craft foam into 1×8–inch strips.

2. Place the sticky-back Velcro onto the ends the foam strips so that they can be folded into circles.

3. If you want the Velcro to be extremely secure so it's less likely to pull loose from the craft foam, you can always adhere it with a dot of hot glue.

4. Print the "ABC Foam Chain" printable letters, cut the letters out, and glue one onto the center of each foam chain. Here's a tip: print the letters onto sticker paper so they easily stick to the craft foam strips.

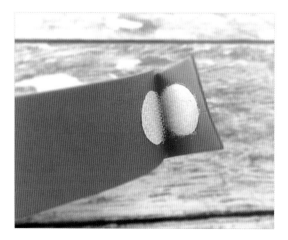

Spring

CUPCAKE SIDEWALK CHALK

Spring is the perfect time to color beautiful pictures outside with sidewalk chalk! This Cupcake Sidewalk Chalk takes drawing outside to a whole new level! It looks exactly like a frosted cupcake but draws exactly like regular sidewalk chalk. You can put sprinkles on top, wrap it in some cellophane, and make it a unique gift or party favor. Cupcake Sidewalk Chalk takes a little bit of time to make, but the extra fun chalk will last a long time!

Supplies Needed

- cupcake tin
- white cupcake liners
- measuring cup
- plaster of Paris
- warm water
- disposable bowls or containers
- plastic spoons
- tempera paint (brown and pink)
- disposable frosting decorating bags
- star-shaped frosting tip
- sprinkles (optional)

Directions

1. Line a cupcake tin with 4–5 cupcake liners

2. Combine ½ cup of plaster of Paris with ¼ cup of warm water in a disposable container.

3. Stir with a plastic spoon until the clumps are gone and the mixture is smooth.

4. Add in 2 tablespoons of brown tempera paint (one at a time to achieve desired color).

5. When the mixture becomes a little thick, gently pour it into the cupcake liners.

6. Let the brown "cake" part of the chalk dry overnight.

Directions Continued

7. Once the cake chalk is completely dry, you can begin making the frosting part of the chalk.

8. Repeat steps 2–4, but add in pink tempera paint instead.

9. Before the mixture becomes too thick, pour it into a disposable frosting bag prepared with a star-shaped frosting tip. (The chalk mixture thickens quickly, so you do need to work fast!)

10. When the mixture achieves a frosting-like thickness, gently frost the top of the cupcake chalk.

11. Shake some sprinkles on top of the wet chalk frosting (optional).

12. Clean the frosting tip before the chalk mixture dries.

13. Let the frosting part of the chalk dry overnight.

14. When both the cake and the frosting sections of the chalk are dry, they will fall right out of the cupcake tin, and you can begin coloring beautiful creations outside!

STEP 2–4

STEP 10

STEP 13

DIY LIP BALM

Handmade lip balm is one of my favorite things to make, and it works incredibly well! It is a perfect gift for others too. Not only is it a great moisturizer for dry lips, it's also super fun to make. The ingredients are perfect for keeping your lips healthy during cold or warm weather. This tutorial makes about 4 tubes of lip balm. You can find empty lip balm containers and the ingredients at some health food stores, or you can buy them online. If you have food coloring, the color possibilities are endless! Because this tutorial involves heating the ingredients, parent supervision is needed.

Supplies Needed

- beeswax
- shea butter
- coconut oil
- glass or disposable bowls
- red food coloring (optional)
- disposable plastic pipettes
- lip balm tubes or jars
- "Heart" lip printable labels
- sticky paper

FIND THE PRINTABLE AT
CEDARFORTBOOKS.COM/SMARTSCHOOLHOUSE

Directions

1. Combine 2 tablespoons of grated beeswax, 3 tablespoons of shea butter, and 2 tablespoons of coconut oil in a glass or disposable bowl. (Parent guidance advised when grating beeswax.)

2. Next, an adult can melt the ingredients together in a microwave in 30-second intervals, stirring between intervals. Stirring will help the ingredients melt together so less heating is needed.

3. Add 1 drop of red food coloring into the melted mixture and stir until completely combined. Or add whatever colors you are excited to make!

Spring

Directions Continued

4. Using a disposable pipette, transfer the melted mixture to lip balm tubes (or pour it into lip balm jars).

5. Let the melted mixture harden for about 20 minutes, and you are done!

6. Print the heart labels on sticky paper (like shipping or address labels), and place them on the lids of your lip balm containers.

STEP 1

STEP 4

LUCKY SHAMROCK WANDS

We need all the luck we can get on St. Patrick's Day! That's why these lil' Lucky Shamrock Wands will come in handy. Make them a couple of days before St. Patrick's Day so they are ready to use when the big leprechaun hunt happens. They make searching for four-leaf clovers and leprechauns an almost guaranteed success! They also make fun party decorations. Leprechauns are drawn to gold, and these wands have just enough gold to lure in a lucky leprechaun on St. Patrick's Day!

Supplies Needed

- white craft foam
- tacky glue
- green paint in 3–4 different shades
- paint brushes
- cake pop sticks
- gold ribbon

Directions

1. Trace 3 hearts on the white craft foam.

2. Glue the hearts together on the sides to create a shamrock shape.

3. When the glue is dry, paint them using different shades of green.

4. When the shamrocks are dry, glue them to a cake pop stick.

5. Glue 2-inch-long gold ribbon streamers to the back of each shamrock.

Spring

STEP 1

STEP 2

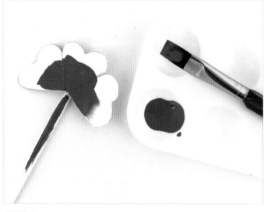

STEP 3

STEP 4

STEP 5

DIY CELL PHONE STAND

Here's a fun cell phone stand that would make a fun gift for a teacher. It's also the perfect Mother's Day gift. While you can buy cell phone docks and stands commercially, creating your own is so much more fun! You can add personal touches including your choice of colors and design. It's a gift that's pretty and practical. What I love about this project is that it involves a combination of painting and scrapbook paper. Those two things create an endless possibility of stylish outcomes!

Supplies Needed

- an unfinished wood plaque stand (found at a craft store)
- scrapbook paper
- scissors
- Mod Podge glue
- unfinished wood accessories, picket fence
- acrylic pant in your colors of choice
- sponge paintbrushs
- wood glue

Directions

1. Start by tracing the shape of the outside edge of the unfinished wood plaque onto scrapbook paper of your choice. Next, cut out the traced shape.

2. Paint a thin layer of Mod Podge onto the surface of your wood plaque, and adhere the scrapbook paper to the plaque surface. Let it dry for a few minutes.

3. Paint a thin layer of Mod Podge all over the surface of the scrapbook paper you just attached to the wood plaque. This layer of glue on top helps seal the scrapbook paper into place!

Directions Continued

4. Paint the other unfinished wood embellishments you picked out using acrylic paint. I chose to paint a white picket fence.

5. Glue your painted wood embellishments onto the wood plaque with wood glue.

6. Let the wood glue, paint, and Mod Podge dry completely.

STEP 1

STEP 2

STEP 3

STEP 4

STEP 5

Directions Continued

7. Set your cell phone and even your cell phone charger in the cell phone stand! It creates a stylish, fun, and organized spot for your phone.

STEP 6

FROSTED CUPCAKE HAND SOAP
For the Sweet Hands of Teachers

Did you know that you can make your very own hand soap? It's a very simple tutorial, but the best part is that with a little added fragrance oil, you can make it smell like so many wonderful things! For this particular hand soap, we are going to use frosted cupcake fragrance oil (or cupcake fragrance oil). You can find a variety of different skin-safe fragrance oils, hand soap containers, and liquid castile soap online or at your favorite drugstore. This Frosted Cupcake Hand Soap has a special label that you can print and wrap up for your teacher in a large muffin cake liner. She will be so impressed with your yummy creation!

Supplies Needed

- mixing bowl
- measuring cups
- distilled water
- liquid castile soap (fragrance free)
- frosted cupcake fragrance oil
- empty hand soap container
- "Frosted Cupcake Hand Soap" printable label
- sticky paper

> FIND THE PRINTABLE AT
> CEDARFORTBOOKS.COM/SMARTSCHOOLHOUSE

Directions

1. In a mixing bowl, combine 1 cup of distilled water with 1 cup of castile soap.

2. Add in 1 or 2 drops of frosted cupcake fragrance oil. The oil is very potent, so be sure you don't use too much!

3. Stir the ingredients together gently without creating too many bubbles.

4. Transfer the mixture to an empty soap container.

5. Print the "Frosted Cupcake Hand Soap" label on sticky paper (like a shipping label) and apply it to the dry hand soap container.

frosted cupcake

HAND SOAP

for the sweet hands of teachers

to ....

............from

HAWAIIAN PUNCH—DYED EASTER EGGS

Creating beautifully colorful Easter eggs is one of my favorite things to do in the spring! But, did you know that you don't have to use smelly dyes? I've learned that a common drink powder contains the perfect ingredients to dye Easter eggs! Hawaiian Punch is a classic juice, and now you can purchase them in single-serve packets. This is perfect for dying Easter eggs! The colors are vibrant, and best of all, they smell sugary sweet!

Supplies Needed

- water
- individual packets of single-serve Hawaiian Punch juice mix (flavors/colors of choice)
- small bowls
- hardboiled eggs
- spoons
- napkins or a drying rack

Directions

1. Combine ½ cup of water with 1 packet of Hawaiian Punch juice mix in a small bowl.

2. Stir until the powder is completely dissolved.

3. Place a hardboiled egg into the bowl. Periodically rotate the eggs to achieve even coloring.

4. When the desired hue is reached, remove the egg, and let it dry on a paper towel or drying rack.

STEP 1

STEPS 1–2

Spring

STEP 3

— HERE'S A TIP —

The longer the eggs sit in the Hawaiian Punch juice, the more vibrant the colors will be!

SPARKLING BUNNY FOOTPRINT ROCKS

The kids and I always have fun discovering ways to celebrate spring through crafts. These Sparkling Bunny Footprint Rocks turn out perfectly every time! Collect some small rocks outside (little kids are really good at doing this), gather your craft supplies, and begin creating footprint masterpieces. The Sparkling Bunny Footprint Rocks will each take on a personality of their own! Add sparkles, and place them outside for the spring sun to shine down on. Anyone who finds them outside is sure to be surprised with your adorable creations!

Supplies Needed

- superglue (with adult help)
- small circular rocks: 6 smaller rocks to make toes and 2 medium-sized rocks for paw bases
- paint brushes
- white acrylic paint
- acrylic in pastel colors (or your colors of choice)
- white glue
- coordinating fine glitter colors

Directions

1. Parents: using superglue, glue 3 smaller rocks to 1 medium rock to create a footprint shape. Repeat, depending on how many footprint pairs you plan to make.

2. Paint the paws with a white acrylic base. Let dry.

3. Paint the paw pairs in various pastel colors. Let dry. Repeat with additional coats of color if necessary.

Directions Continued

4. Paint a thin layer of white glue over the dried paint.

5. Add glitter to the wet glue.

6. Let the Sparkling Bunny Footprint Rocks completely dry, and then arrange them outside in bunny-like footprint paths. Store in a dry, cool place.

STEP 1

STEP 4

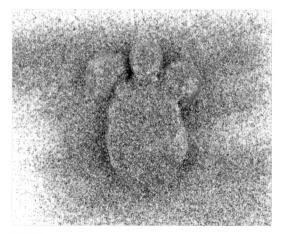

STEP 5

STEP 6

Summer

LEMONADE STAND

Hosting a lemonade stand is a summer rite of passage—especially for the budding entrepreneur! Not only do you need to create the perfect lemonade recipe, but you also need to have a smart system for keeping track of your sales! This activity includes printable straw toppers, a sales record, and receipts to give to your customers. Practicing how to count back change is a great skill, and it is a great way to keep your math skills sharp during the summer. With all of these supplies, you are bound to have the best-selling lemonade stand on the block!

Supplies Needed

- "Lemonade Stand" printable straw toppers
- scissors
- paper or plastic straws
- double-sided tape
- "Sales Record" printable
- "Lemonade Receipts" printable

FIND THE PRINTABLE AT
CEDARFORTBOOKS.COM/SMARTSCHOOLHOUSE

Directions

1. Print the "Lemonade Stand" straw toppers on plain white paper. Cut them out and attach them to straws using double-sided tape.

2. To use the Lemonade Receipts, multiply the number of cups you sold to each customer by the cost per cup. For example: 3 cups × $1 per cup. Write down the answer on the "Total" line.

3. To find the "Change Due," subtract the "Amount Received" by the "Total."

4. Write down how much change you owe them back on the "Change Due" line.

5. Record the "Customer Number," the "# of Cups Purchased" by the customer, and the "Sale Total" on the Sales Record sheet.

6. When you are ready to close up shop for the day, calculate your grand total by adding up all of the totals on your Sales Record.

ICE CREAM PLAY DOUGH

Do your kids like ice cream? Do your kids like play dough? Let's combine those two wonderful things into a kid-friendly craft that is sure to provide lots of smiles and giggles! Ice Cream Play Dough will change the way you look at homemade play dough recipes forever! It is fun, it moves, it scoops, and it shapes just like ice cream. The best part is that it is completely edible! Two simple ingredients will provide hours and hours of play.

Supplies Needed

- an electric mixer with a dough paddle attachment
- premade frosting in your flavor(s) of choice
- powdered sugar
- olive oil (as needed)
- ice cream cones, ice cream scoop, bowls, and other play dough toys (optional)

STEP 1

Directions

1. Using an electric mixer and a dough paddle attachment, slowly combine 1 cup of pre-made frosting with 2¾ cups of powdered sugar. (Reserve the last ¼ cup of powdered sugar until after you have tested the consistency of the finished play dough.)

2. Beat, continually scraping the sides of the bowl.

3. Premade frostings vary a bit, so it's best to test the "stickiness" of your play dough as you add in the powdered sugar. Before you add the last ¼ cup of the powdered sugar, touch the play dough and, if it feels sticky, add the rest of the powered sugar in.

Directions Continued

4. Roll it into one big ball and make sure it is not crumbly or sticky. If you added a little too much powdered sugar, sprinkle a little olive oil onto the play dough. Olive oil will help prevent the play dough from drying out as you play with it too.

5. Store the ice cream play dough in a ziplock bag in the refrigerator. It will harden in the refrigerator, so when you want to play with it again, take it out of the refrigerator and let it sit for 30 minutes or until it reaches room temperature.

6. Sprinkle a little olive oil onto the dough and get right back to playing!

CAKE POP MARSHMALLOW SHOOTERS

Here's a fun, active project for a warm summer afternoon. Turn an average cake pop container into a marshmallow shooting game, and who knows what type of competition you could create? Mini marshmallows are fun to eat, but this inexpensive and entertaining tool turns them into "ammunition" you'll use for creating summer memories and getting in a little bit of active play time. Use your mini launcher, made with a balloon and a cake pop container, to launch marshmallows into the air and toward other predetermined targets. You could even take turns trying to catch the marshmallows in your mouths. Pick teams, play solo, or surprise someone when they're least expecting it!

Supplies needed

- balloons
- scissors
- plastic cake pop containers
- mini marshmallows

Directions

1. Tie the end of an empty balloon into a knot.

2. Cut the balloon in half (as pictured).

3. Remove the lid and the stick from a cake pop container.

4. Place the tied end of the balloon over the cake pop container.

Directions Continued

5. Place a mini marshmallow down into the cake pop container where the stick normally goes.

6. With one hand on the cake pop container and one hand on the balloon tie, pull back on the balloon tie and quickly let it go, launching the mini marshmallow into the air.

STEP 2

STEP 5

MAGNETIC WATERMELON SEED COUNTING

Counting, patterning, and practicing other math skills is important during long summer breaks from school. Finding creative ways to keep your math skills sharp is the fun part. This activity creates a magnetic watermelon out of a metal pizza pan. Small black magnetics look just like watermelon seeds and are perfect for counting practice. You can count seeds, create patterns with seeds, or even make silly shapes and pictures with them!

Supplies Needed

- pencil
- metal pizza pan
- scissors
- red construction paper
- white glue
- green construction paper
- small round magnets

Directions

1. Trace ½ of the inside of the pizza pan with red construction paper.

2. Cut out the half-circle shape and glue it to the pizza pan.

3. Trace ½ of the outer edge of the pizza pan onto green construction paper. Using this shape, freehand draw a 1-inch thick green rind.

4. Cut it out and glue it to the outer edge of your pizza pan.

5. Use small black magnets to create watermelon seeds. Practice addition, subtraction, pattern making, or even picture making with your magnetic watermelon seeds.

Summer

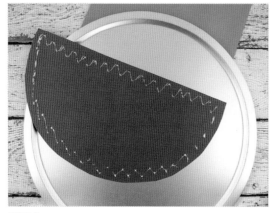

STEP 2

STEP 3

STEP 5

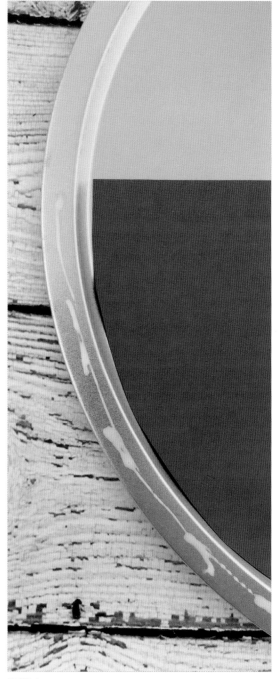

STEP 4

COOLING SUMMER LEI

Summer is hot! For those days when you aren't playing in a pool or at the beach, crafting up a Cooling Summer Lei is a great way to beat the heat! Wear it around your neck and let it cool you down on a scorching hot summer day. You can even get super creative and make bracelets, rings, or anklets if you want! They are reusable and fun to make with friends.

Supplies Needed

- scissors
- colored sponges (without a rough scrubbing side)
- flat plastic craft string
- ice cube tray

Directions

1. Cut the colored sponges into small squares.

2. Using double knots, continually tie the sponge squares along a long piece of flat plastic craft string.

3. Measure the length of the lei as you go, and cut according to your desired length.

Directions Continued

4. Place each sponge on your lei into the individual compartments of the ice cube tray.

5. Pour a little bit of water over the sponges in the ice cube tray. No need to drench the sponges! Your sponges only need to absorb enough water to make them damp.

6. Put the ice cube tray into the freezer and take it out when the sponges are frozen.

7. Tie the lei around your neck and head outside! You'll love how cool your Cooling Summer Lei makes you feel!

BEACH BALL HOT AIR BALLOONS

A beach ball is a summertime staple, and this craft turns a regular beach ball into something extra fun! Even if you've never been on a hot air balloon ride, this project will make you excited for one in the future! You can use the Beach Ball Hot Air Balloons as summer party decor or you can hang them in your room. We actually have ours hanging in our playroom, and they add the perfect playful touch during the summer.

Supplies Needed

- scissors
- string
- tacky glue
- small, white popcorn or treat boxes
- beach balls
- fishing line
- thumbtacks or damage-free mini picture frame hooks

Directions

1. Cut 4 pieces of string 2 feet long each (or to desired length). Repeat for desired number of hot air balloons.

2. Glue the string ends to the 4 sides of the treat boxes and let dry.

3. Glue the other ends of the 4 strings to the top of the blown up beach balls. (The top part is the nozzle.) Let dry.

4. Cut a piece of fishing line and string it through the air nozzle at the top of the balloon. Tie the fishing line in a knot to secure it.

5. Have a grown-up help tie the other end of the fishing line to a thumbtack.

Directions Continued

6. Hang the hot air balloons from the ceiling by pushing the thumbtacks into the ceiling, or use damage-free clear mini picture frame hooks adhered directly to the ceiling with fishing line tied around the hook.

RED, WHITE, AND BLUE ICE PACKS

Whether you fall down and need an ice pack to help you feel better, or you want to dress up a patriotic ice chest with something different, these Red, White, and Blue Ice Packs are sure to catch the attention of others! Did you know that it is actually very simple to make your own ice packs? They stay soft enough to calm down a hurting knee or elbow, but they also keep lunch boxes and ice buckets cool too. I just love that! Add a little glitter, and these ice packs are perfect for your patriotic party.

Supplies Needed

- red and blue food coloring
- sandwich-size ziplock plastic bags
- red, white, and blue craft glitter
- measuring cup
- water
- rubbing alcohol

Directions

1. Put 1 drop of red or blue food coloring into the bag.

2. Sprinkle in some coordinating glitter.

3. Combine 1½ cups of water with ½ cup of rubbing alcohol inside the bag.

4. Seal the bag, and then place another bag over it. The double bag helps keep everything a little more secure.

5. Repeat for each desired color ice pack.

6. Place the ice packs in the freezer until frozen.

7. When the ice packs are melted, put them back in the freezer and reuse them!

Summer

GLOW-IN-THE-DARK WIFFLE BALLS

Something that I adore about summer is that the days are longer. Summer also usually means that we don't have to be at school the next day, so we can stay up later at night! With evening BBQs, the Fourth of July, Labor Day, and so much more, we are often outside, enjoying the warm evening air. These Glow-in-the-Dark Wiffle Balls are a fun way to keep the daytime games going after the summer sun sets! Here's a tip: you can find all of the supplies for this activity at a dollar store.

Supplies Needed

- glow stick bracelets in various colors
- plastic Wiffle balls

Directions

1. When the sun has set, remove the glow sticks from their packaging.

2. Discard the glow stick bracelet connectors.

3. Bend each bracelet to activate the glowing color.

4. Push 2–4 glow stick bracelets into each wiffle ball, making sure that the ends are secured inside and not poking out. This will take a little bit of force and manipulation of the bracelets, but continue to push one end of the glow stick bracelet into the ball, and it will fold and bend accordingly.

5. Take the Glow-in-the-Dark Wiffle Balls outside at night and have fun!

GIGGLE FORMULA FOR TEACHERS

Do you ever feel like your classroom could use a giggle or two? Are you looking for a fun and unique gift to make for your teacher? This gently-scented Giggle Formula is sure to put a smile on a teacher's face and will cheer up a classroom full of hardworking students. Do you want to know what makes this formula so fun? It smells like bubble gum! When kids are feeling sleepy, when a big test is completed, or when a little humorous relief is needed, spritz some Giggle Formula into the air and watch the mood instantly lift! This works especially well in preschool to third-grade classrooms.

Supplies Needed

- empty spray bottle
- distilled water
- bubble gum fragrance oil (available online)
- "Giggle Formula" printable tag
- sticky paper

FIND THE PRINTABLE AT
CEDARFORTBOOKS.COM/SMARTSCHOOLHOUSE

Directions

1. Fill up an empty spray bottle with distilled water.

2. Add 1 or 2 drops of bubble gum fragrance oil to the water. (Fragrance oil can be found easily online.)

3. Close the bottle and give it a shake.

4. Print the "Giggle Formula" tag onto sticky paper and place on the spray bottle.

5. Shake the bottle before each use, and spray 1 or 2 pumps up in the air. The calm yet fun scent of bubble gum will fill the room!

APPLE SUNCATCHERS

Have you ever noticed how beautiful the sun is during the fall? Sunlight filtering through colored leaves or shining its late-afternoon gold rays across the autumn landscape reminds us that the days will soon be getting shorter. There is just something about the leaves changing colors and the smell of fall in the air. Autumn apple-picking season is especially unbeatable! Celebrate the beautiful colors of fall with these apple-shaped suncatchers. Hang them in your room or even in your kitchen. They cast a beautiful red light as they capture the fall sun's rays.

Supplies Needed

- Mason canning jar rings, any desired size(s)
- black pen
- red cellophane
- scissors
- fishing line
- hot glue (with adult help) or regular glue.
- green silk leaves

Directions

1. Remove the flat metal sealing lid from the canning jar rings. You'll only need the "ring" part of the lid.

2. Using a black pen, trace the circle of the outer canning jar lid onto the red cellophane.

3. Cut out the traced circle from the red cellophane.

4. Knot a piece of fishing line through the canning jar lid. Leave enough fishing line to hang the lid later on (about 2 feet).

5. Using hot glue, have a parent adhere the red cellophane circles to the inside of the jar lids. Or use regular glue, but allow for a longer drying time.

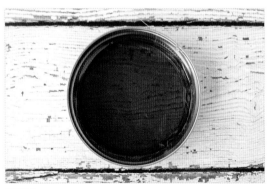

STEP 3

Fall

Directions Continued

6. Glue a green silk leaf to the top of the jar lid.

7. When they are dry, hang your Apple Suncatchers in a window!

APPLE PENCIL HOLDER

When back-to-school season hits, it's all about apples and new school supplies! A fun gift that you can make for your teacher or your friends is a small glass apple pencil holder. They are cool to make, and they look just like little apples! The best part about starting this craft is that you're forced to drink some apple juice before you start. (I secretly love that part!) This Apple Pencil Holder is an adorable way to celebrate a new school year!

Supplies Needed

- sphere-shaped glass apple juice jar
- red acrylic paint
- disposable plates or wax paper for drying
- nail file
- raffia
- tacky glue (or glue gun with parental supervision)
- silk leaf
- new pencils

Directions

1. Clean the inside of a sphere-shaped glass apple juice jar.

2. Fill the jar with red acrylic paint. Swirl the paint around so that all of the glass is covered.

3. When your apple is completely covered in red paint, place the apple upside down on a disposable plate or a plate covered with wax paper so that the excess paint will drain out.

4. Let the apple dry overnight.

STEP 2

Fall

Directions Continued

5. When the paint is completely dry, use a nail file to remove any of the rough paint around the lid of the jar.

6. Wrap raffia around the top of the apple jar and secure with glue.

7. Glue a green silk leaf on top of the raffia.

8. Place new pencils inside!

STEP 2

STEP 3

STEPS 3–4

STEP 5

STEP 6

STEP 7

STEP 8

FIND THE PRINTABLE AT
CEDARFORTBOOKS.COM/SMARTSCHOOLHOUSE

Fall

BUBBLE POTION

Spooky crafts are so fun to create during Halloween! Bubble Potion is perfect for Halloween parties or for an afternoon of festive fun. Turn the potion green (or even black or red), put the potion in a fun clear container, and the kids in the neighborhood will be curious about what you've made. Lucky for you, this is actually very simple to create, which makes it a great craft if you have a group of kids around! With just 2 ingredients and a special "Bubble Potion" tag, you are set for some spooky bubble-blowing fun!

Supplies Needed

- Regular bubbles with wands (I like to buy bubbles from a dollar store.)
- A clear container (Craft stores often sell fun containers.)
- Green food coloring (or food coloring of choice)
- Pipe cleaners (optional)
- "Bubble Potion" printable tag
- Hole punch
- Green-and-white baker's twine

Directions

1. Pour regular bubble solution into a fun-shaped clear container.

2. Add 1–4 drops of food coloring to the bubble solution.

3. Reuse the same bubble wands, or create a new bubble wand one by bending the ends of pipe cleaners into a small circles.

4. Print the "Bubble Potion" printable tag, cut it out, punch a hole at the top, and tie it to your Bubble Potion container with baker's twine.

SPONGE ROLLER SPIDERS

Little kids love to play with fake spiders, and these little sponge roller spiders are so innocent and sweet that even the youngest kiddos will be able to make them! Who knew old-fashioned sponge hair rollers could be used to make spiders for Halloween? They can even double as pencil toppers or finger puppets. I like to tie them with fishing line so they look like they are crawling up and down the walls. Give them names and introduce the spiders to each other. These Sponge Roller Spiders will take on a personality of their own.

Supplies Needed

- black sponge rollers
- scissors
- black pipe cleaners
- various colored googly eyes
- white glue

Directions

1. Remove the sponge rollers from their plastic fasteners.

2. Cut the pipe cleaners into equal pieces for the spider's eight legs. The side of the spider legs can vary depending on what you want your spider to look like. Adult scissors will easily cut through the small wire of pipe cleaners.

3. Using regular white glue (or hot glue to save time), attach four legs to each side of the sponge roller.

4. Glue the googly eyes on one end of the sponge roller.

5. Gently bend the eight legs to allow the spider to stand up.

SPOOKY PINWHEEL DECORATIONS

Aren't these Halloween pinwheels adorable? With a few simple supplies, including paper straws, googly eyes, scrapbook paper, and glue, you've got everything you need to make a perfectly spooky kid-friendly craft. Making pinwheels can become addicting—plus you can modify the accessories for any season of the year. (I love smart crafts like that!) These pinwheels make colorfully spooky Halloween decor for any party, home, or classroom. They also make great party favors or fall gift-wrap accents.

Supplies Needed

- construction paper
- scissors
- ruler
- white glue (or hot glue with adult help)
- googly eyes
- paper straws

Directions

1. Cut paper into squares, 3×3 inches.

2. Lightly draw an X across the square using a ruler.

3. Cut ¾ of the way toward the center on each line. Don't cut all the way into the center.

STEPS 3–4

Directions Continued

4. Bend every other corner into the center of the square, using a teeny tiny dab of glue (white or hot glue) each time.

5. Glue 1 or 2 googly eyes on the center of each pinwheel.

6. Glue the spooky pinwheels to paper straws.

FLAMELESS FALL LUMINARIES

While regular candles aren't necessarily kid-friendly, there are so many fun things you can do with flameless tea lights! These flameless fall luminaries are a perfect gift. Or you can use them to enhance your fall decor. Turn them on as the sun gets close to setting, and the autumn light they create will amaze you. Glowing fall leaves are simply beautiful! Make several at a time to really set a festive scene! What I love the most is that you can use them year after year.

Supplies Needed

- flameless tea lights
- silk fall leaves (3 leaves per tea light)
- glue
- scissors

Directions

1. Cut the stems and the very bottom off of each leaf to create a straight line.

2. Glue the leaf around the base of the tea light. Hold in place until the glue is secure.

3. Repeat step 2 with the other leaves until the flameless candle is covered.

4. Turn on the flameless candles and watch how the candles capture the color of the fall leaves! Wrap them up as gifts or enjoy them in your own home.

EXSTRAW SPECIAL NAPKIN HOLDER
For Thanksgiving

Thanksgiving is a wonderful time to show your friends and family members how grateful you are to know them. Handmade gifts are a great way to show someone that you care. Decorate each place setting at your Thanksgiving table with these handmade Thanksgiving napkin holders. This fun activity strengthens fine motor skills and provides pattern-making practice. The finished napkin holders add a handmade touch to the Thanksgiving table and bring some festive color to each place setting.

Supplies Needed

- scissors
- string
- plastic straws (2 red, 2 orange, and 2 yellow)
- cloth napkin
- silk leaf
- "ExStraw Special Guest" printable tags
- double-sided tape

Directions

1. Cut a piece of string 1 foot long.

2. Cut the red, orange, and yellow straws into pieces (½-inch works well).

3. Create a repeating pattern by stringing the straw pieces together.

4. Tie the string of straws around a cloth napkin. Wrap it around until it is snugly in place and secure it with a knot.

5. Tuck a silk leaf behind the straws on the napkin.

6. Print out an "ExStraw Special Guest" tag and attach it to the bottom of the leaf using double-sided tape.

FIND THE PRINTABLE AT
CEDARFORTBOOKS.COM/SMARTSCHOOLHOUSE

ABOUT THE AUTHOR

Mom, teacher, and successful blogger Kelly Dixon has a passion for making learning fun and creative. Her easy-to-understand projects are designed for children, parents, and teachers. Kelly embraces the combination of education and creativity to help children and families lead positive, happy, and smart lives. Her work has been recognized by Disney, *Good Housekeeping*, MSN, *What to Expect When You're Expecting*, *The Huffington Post*, and more. Kelly resides with her husband and children along the coast of south Orange County, California.